The
Necessary
Boat

The Necessary Boat

Susan Baran

THE GROUNDWATER PRESS
Hudson

PAINTED LEAF PRESS
New York City

A co-publication of the Groundwater Press and Painted Leaf Press.

Cover Painting, "Georgica Pond: Big Sail," by Cornelia Foss.
Book Design by Brian Brunius.
Printed in Canada

ACKNOWLEDGEMENTS

Grateful acknowledgement is made to the editors of the publications in which some of these poems first appeared: "Midterm in Harlem" and "The Spelling Test" in *Poetry New York;* "Among Nightingales" and "Optical Illusion" in *Private 6;* "Bracelet" in *Chelsea;* "Escape" and "Optical Illusion" in *HeadJus.com;* "Gravity" in *Blood & Tears: Poems for Matthew Shepard;* "One Vision" in *At Home with Art.*

Many thanks to Marc Cohen for his constant and invaluable support.

Library of Congress Cataloging-in-Publication Data

Baran, Susan.
   The necessary boat / Susan Baran.
      p.   cm.
   ISBN 1-891305-19-0
   I. Title
PS3552.A5913N43 2000
811' . 54–dc21

                                     99-41318
                                       CIP

*To the memory of my mother, Catherine
and my father, Stanley*

Table of Contents

I

II

III

IV

About the Author

I

Brick Kiln Road

I have seen the golden wheat
weaving in the wind
like the dancer's seven veils;
witnessed mountain laurel
riot in pale pink bursts
ambushing cedars and firs
while the sun called green echoes.

I have come time and time
again to the dark portal,
losing the forward
thrust of the future—
gaining the intensity of now.
I am a captive,
a supplicant
at the altar of technology.

Yesterday, they harvested
my brave wheat.
Cropped stems are all that remain
along with the memory of a defiant beauty,
pious spikes punctuating the mossy hills of summer.
It has vanished, I do not know where—
like the life I used to lead,
the one measured in ordinary hours.

Optical Illusion

The holy intake, outtake
of breath made visible
by the solidifying chill,
the sun so urgently branding
flesh and field in July
now merely gilt paint.
Snow sings with cool diamond
fire as tongues of flame
etch the sentinel pines,
their evergreen points
the only reminder of that other
season's color scheme.

The visitors follow all instructions—
bleed the silver-finned radiators,
rejoice over the orchestration
of steam rising through angled pipes.
They miss dog and master
whose presence is felt
in every nook and cranny.
Even though the sinewy pooch
is seventy miles distant,
the soft cushions inside her blue armchair
remain arranged along familiar contours
like the force field at the poles.

It's only when the adjustment
of valves and gauges is complete
and the house has begun to offer
its paintings, books and poems
on their most intimate terms

that they discover the cracked
and broken pane in the outer
dining room entrance. City thoughts
of break-ins percolate,
a closer look reveals
the corpse of a beautiful bird
neither can name
lodged between the inner and storm doors.

Soft brown with gray wing tips
and blue specks—its belly has been slit
by the glass spears
of the fragmented portal,
greenish bile stains its underside.
Straightening up they are blinded
by the sun boring through
the facing window—the pristine house
erased, the opposite of a mirage—
they don't see what's actually there,
like so many before and yet to come.

One Vision

for Georgia O'Keeffe

What need have I of color
except that which clings
to the blue sky or streaked clay
of the desert? I hoard the finest
oils in tubes, mix and re-mix
to capture the energy of this planet,
the light that dances
and darts from each object.
I want the form of tears,
not their melancholy.

The earth is constant.
We crave the color that surrounds us,
steal the last, pink drop of sunset
for a scarf to wrap our throat,
wear a skirt of plum that hugs pale hips.
Clothed in radiance and desire
we pluck the sacred day.
I want none of this—
I am content in black and white,
all absence, all presence.

Only the joy of canvas
helps me see a little clearer
each time I paint, that others
may know on dove gray walls
in a city shaded by towers,
obscured by the mist of a million breaths,
the stars that shine above the desert.
My pictures exist only
for a brief moment in this world,

then they dry and bleach
like the bones whose scattered figures
haunt these sands, and when I too
have turned to bone, form will join form
in the order of this universe.
I will be that which I have struggled
to know through my fingertips, to see—
smooth and polished into final form
like the black river rock that rests
on a white shelf above my bed,
I shall be alone and pure.

Barnard Greenhouse

Nervous winds blow wild
as storms roll in.
Incandescent discharges
shock the sky.
We are red ants
circling the miniature
citrus forest, while in another room
a scientist varies the temperature
of the soil to see the effect,
if any, on the sweet potato.
Young Bryan writes
in his field journal,
"What an insect needs to survive
is for a man not to step on it."

Delta of New York
radiates down the Hudson.
Late afternoon sun stipples
rooftops and the giant machinery
that keeps the internal order
cooking and cooling
for mundane and sacred pursuits.
Glass cap on an ordinary
university building—
within clear walls, scents
and colors are designed
to seduce pollinators.

In the small, square office,
a stained table surrounded

by four functional ancient chairs—
the natural and manipulated,
each with their distinct beauty.
The Venus flytrap will not
be closed by random touch,
but requires a double tap
to prime its trap—
a strange respect for life in
its most lethal form.

Haunted Horizon

The blood of America's first
transoceanic settlers
roils in besieged veins—
diluted by desire
and the geometric progression
of future generations.
Thunderheads marbleize the vista
above the stubborn curving coast.

Once a childhood foray
into masses of my mother's fifties beads
excavated a tiny crystal star—
symbol of the Daughters
of the American Revolution,
full of history and assumption.
Beacon of a time
before supplemental homes
fragmented the low-
slung hump of the harbor.

Each angle of recollection
opens forgotten firmaments.
The glazed waters
sigh with repeated events.
Telescoping blue eyes
scan the beach—
speeding snapshots
fuse into the wider necessary view
of the continent's rim
as the sands accept
accumulation and loss.

The Spelling Test

Sometimes spelling she was writing
white answers on blackboards.
The white answers became gray answers
inside thirty-two marbled notebooks.
The thirty-two marbled notebooks having
many pages there was much erasing
of old white answers. This was done
by monitors. When the erasers stopped
accepting old white answers, they were taken
downstairs. All thirty-two of the marbled notebooks
wanted to be the ones feeding
old white answers to the eraser cleaner.
Only two could be doing this at one time.
The rest of the marbled notebooks
sat listening to a story about taking turns,
knowing this was not even a white answer.
On Fridays, the gray answers inside
the thirty-two marbled notebooks were written
on yellow papers with blue lines.
This writing was done without looking
inside the marbled notebooks.
Looking inside a marbled notebook could get
a yellow paper with blue lines a red zero,
no matter how many fine gray answers
it was holding. On Fridays, the blackboards
having no white answers—this was not easy.

Paradise

for John Ash

The women of Byzantium find
an advocate along the Mersey.

An obscure composer squashes the cat.
God is replaced by a compact disc.

In the capital, the Potato Institute
pays homage to variations on a sweet tuber.

The American experience includes a stint
as Hansel in the forest of parties.

A little girl is exhilarated by the fact
that *he* is taller than her mother.

The Milky Way unveils itself
above a dancing class for trees

as spidery cuneiform weaves the anomaly
the information age is gunning for.

The Necessary Boat

Banished by my father
to escape Napoleon's
military expectations,
smuggled to the harbor
of America's commerce,
always the lessons
of the outdoors sang to me.
Scholarship or business
could not compete
with the comfort of bird or bloom,
extant forests, just beginning
to feel the swipe of civilization's ax.

I cuffed silver thread
around the legs
of a pair of phoebes,
the better to recognize
if indeed, spring brings
a return to familiar nests.
Others thought
feathered beings hibernated
underwater or in hollow trees.
Later, they called it banding,
a way to know who
comes and goes.
No harm done
in the name
of science, this time.

Those first crude drawings
when I saw the actual birds—
blood rushed to my temples
in despair. To kill, to study—
wires piercing newly
dead bodies, twisted into positions
life had once assumed,
made manifest
the conflict between bird
and beast of human variety.
Passenger pigeons in masses
so great as to defy imagination
would soon disappear from
America's broad skies.

Wilson and his *American Ornithology*
showed me the way
out of debt and into immortality—
a book of all America's birds,
to find and name
the familiar and unsung.
Oh, my constant Lucy—
we dared not guess the hard
path we'd set—the separations,
the doubters, the envious.
I adopted the free clothes
of a frontiersman, the flowing
locks of vanity, left you,
our sons, our dear dead
infant daughters.
I went where the fever
took me—across the continent,
down wide rivers and nameless roads,
always the next bird calling.

I had one hundred
different plans—waged
war against failure.

Ordinary dimensions
would not do, the double
elephant folio—an impossible
size, but the subject,
the effort, demanded it.
At the bottom of each
plate: Drawn from nature
by J. J. Audubon.
A thousand strangers'
portraits painted that I
might send some token,
buy the pencil, hire
the necessary boat.
I drove an iron pen
trying to explain.

Returned to Europe—
sold myself as curiosity, scientist,
artist, whatever whet
their appetite for subscriptions.
The divide between nature's
touch and the currency of man.
The engravers, the colorists,
their genius, their demands.
Backgrounds I learned
to relinquish to others,
economies of plants and settings
for the cormorants, tanagers,
black-throated mango hummingbirds,
the larks and sparrows.
The redoing, the attempt

to make perfect by
the hand of man.
Slowly the pages came.
Would these mortal bones
survive to survey each rookery?

The golden eagle whose beauty
I dared not mar—
its heart pierced with a pin
when all other methods failed.
Thirteen days I labored
at that image.
My hand, my lip, my mouth
palsied afterward, the great
fellow exacting his due.
Glorious days when finally
we were together—you editing,
our sons drawing, selling,
a family making *The Birds of America.*
My legacy, no longer illusion,
Minniesland, our home.
Eyes, then intellect,
began to fail.
My old comrade writes, "Alas, my poor
friend Audubon, the outlines
of his countenance and his form
are there, but his noble
mind is all in ruins."

Among Nightingales

The green, green grass
paints its secrets
over and over in clover.
One self dies so that . . .
I am both and more,
more than the sum of the parts,
less than part of the sum.

Browning feared "the pure, white light"—
the struggle visceral, not intellectual.
James saw—
"alternative presences,
the assertion of either . . .
involved the entire
extinction of the other."

People roam exquisite rooms,
abstinence and decadence their twin deities.
Bruised desires spin the olives.
Who can shut up such a bird?
The moon is a vermilion torch
fusing comedy and tragedy
in a neutral facade.

The mind races before sleep.
Elizabeth prayed, "God,
if there be a God, save
my soul, if I have a soul."
She urged Robert, "the mask thrown off,
however moist with breath."
He asked, "How do I . . . How can I?"

II

Fine Tuning

The shock of it,
puzzled eyes betray
what she does not say to the camera.

Blonde topknot like a question mark;
gray velvet pony, pink yarn mane, imaginary
pigeon coos inside your hand.

Stand for first time braced
by water trickling from garden spigot.

Santa Claus decal
hovering above the kitchen table,
"Better finish, he's watching . . . "

Gold engraved bangle from bachelor
Uncle Joe, your wrist
will outgrow it, but not by much.

Man in Miami buys you comic books,
doesn't register as sex offender.

Turtle's shell lethally softens, flush
down porcelain bowl. Plastic palm
tree never droops.

Packed off to Aunt Olga's while sister
is born. Forced to play catch,
shatter garage door window.

Blessed predictability
of Miss MacMurray's first grade.

Blast the cliff behind apartment
to clear way for shopping center.
Observe action from fire escape.

Dog tags in case North Koreans
expand the war, strafe Bronx.
Chain turns your neck green.

Best friend, Lois Polansky's bread
box door opens spontaneously,
smashes parakeet.

Both children, chicken pox,
husband broken leg, mother
threatens to leave.

Want to be Roy Rogers,
Dale Evans dead-end position.

Tony Home Permanent curls, not.

Parents say no to bicycle,
Davidson Avenue too steep.

Ginny Doll, all accessories
except Barbie's boobs.

Mona's mother postulates
her daughter's obese
because she swallows air.

Love lemon appetite
tonic, no interest in food.

Crack of your ankle like a gunshot
descending four flights.

Cancer, they whisper,
think we can't hear.

Bronx-Lebanon engulfs mother. Dream
of being chased thru dark castle.

Mickey Mouse explains mystery
of menstruation to Girl Scouts.

Five Susans homeroom, two Susan B.'s.

When alone, use lemon juice
to bleach emergent arm hairs.

Finish *Gone with the Wind* in
two days. Only your mother believes you.

Music teacher, white satin blouse,
evils of the constricting brassiere.
Peer Gynt—The Hall of the Mountain King.

Emulate our elders, mah-jongg.
Between racking tiles
read *Peyton Place* aloud.

Little sister makes Yogi and Boo-Boo,
"Oh, what a wonderful pair," commit
unspeakable acts.

The year of all pink clothes.
Sex frees you from the child you were.

Always carry matches
when venturing inside the Girls' Room.

Q-44 Bus, as gateway to another
world. Professor Ray—the Novel
in English Literature.

Do you have the courage?

F. B. I. snaps protesters. Tommy
blown up by a land mine.

Remission ends with a cough.
War on all fronts.

Older, drives a candy-apple-
blue convertible, knows the way
out of the valley of the shadow.

We were not blind but we
did not see. Hysteria
when the priest spills the beans.

That funeral and Neil Armstrong's
giant step the same day.

Ten years to remember shredded
homework, hand prints on your arm.

Oh, Orangeberg, why are the ladies
in full regalia in Waldbaum's?

Lawn King grows more grass
for the boy next door to mow.

Attempt Nanuet Mall,
wind up in Pennsylvania.

Read *The Feminine Mystique.*
Wallpaper makes you tremble.

Turn off TV to get
his attention. Fail.

Skyview, a room of my
own, thank you, Virginia.

"D" word enters vocabulary. Pray
for technology to find a way to save you.

Sometime, someone
before you, but who?

1974 Gremlin folds
like Grandpa Bruno's accordion.

Class 2-8—thirty-three boys, one
girl—going to die in this classroom.

COLUMBIA
MFA

Layout worst case scenario,
he still will not go away.

Sweep of the Hudson, snow
through the bathroom skylight.

Hospital hell commences.
What you don't question can kill.

Hardware store as 1920s Paris,
patrons and poets on paint cans.

Map of bruises, platelets
failing. Trip Tik indicates
this is it, kiddo.

Forty-five, pearls, dialysis,
there I can say it.

Hostage poetry, three days on, four
off. Life support ignores
calendar frivolities.

Raimundo dreams I'm Frieda
Kalho, free arm painting.

Wind tunnel inside the 77th Street Station,
Monday, Wednesday and Friday, 9 P. M.

Promise of replacement part
within two years, better off
than being dead.

Seven months later a call, "We have one,
want it?"

YES YES YES

Cry, cry, cry,
squeezed dry by delirium.

Post-op, day two, ZOOMING.
Museum of Sugar Art.

Fifty pastel parasols aflame
behind you; ahead?

April

for James Schuyler

Begins
in the memory
of March
as buds commence
their journey
to the light.

Nature
can break
your heart.

The cat
does double-time
around
the house
quivering
from head

to paw
as wayward
pigeons
glide past
casement
windows.

Time
divides
along the fault
line where
a person
an epoch
ruptures—

an ordinary
month
marked
forever
by Jimmy's
passing.

In One Place

I draw the drapes against the peak of light.
The sun must never get a chance to act
upon the leather backs of books.

Saffron panes absorb the violet rays
that would corrode my treasures, crumble them
to dust as they sit upon the shelf.

I leave a space between my volumes to repel
the white haunt of mildew that thrives
atop a damp page. The first book

I ever loved was a dictionary
with gilded edges and a black Morocco
cover. Sealed pages stuck

together filled with words for me
to claim. My soul knew other bodies, was not
bound by circumstance, or sex,

or experience. I sought my own
true form while the din of everyday
swirled about my chair. The lives

I've lived panel this study in regimented
rows of polished calf that reach so high
a ladder must be scaled to seize

their secrets. Books are fragile—dust, heat
and worms have no respect for clarity
of text, only passion for the taste

of paper, glue and glair. I do my best
to spare my loves gross indignities.
The oils from fingers stain a bit

each time a page is turned. Yet
leather needs the charity
of contact, the touch of hands.

Corona

Easter, St. Mary's—
founded 1914
by Polish immigrants;

stark white, pure,
unforgiving white; scarlet
vestments, church of blood;

babble of Slavic syllables;
chaos I do not understand.
We only spoke our mother's English tongue.

Blade slices ceiling, guts
oppressive Florida air.
Do not faint.

You can retire here,
from your life,
your children, adopt

a new identity,
or was that other you,
the father we knew, the alias?

My late mother's salt shaker
in stepmother Basha's basket
for the priest to bless.

The deceased's Protestant
soul would not have
indulged in such idolatry.

This paternal Polish
crusade, an enigma.
I am always the pretender

full of silent
stoic thunder.
This is not my sanctuary,

why does it hurt me so?
The worshippers have made
a voyage I cannot

desire or understand.
Is my ungodliness exposed
in this unwavering tropical light?

Hours

Green hills layer
like paint chips.

One limb of a giant butternut
on the brink, victim
of its own accumulated mass.

Dear paper teases.
Will we stumble
upon what we need?

The wood thrush systematically
strips the red berries.

The house, strangely
not itself, chairs
isolate in contemplation.

The rapture of silence.

Material objects deport
themselves as anchors.

Many stories behind
each donned gown.

Hidden life of root and insect.

Clouds open like windows
to another world.

Black Frost

Snow's gossamer sheet
bleaches the night,
usurps dawn's birthright,
as all hours meet
in unnatural conceit.
The moon's kite
relinquishes the limelight
to winter's feat.

Sleepwalk to the kitchen to feed the cat—
around the rims
of window shades
an illuminated lariat
of glitter swims,
guides mute parades.

Orrery

A woman sits on a bench
on a path of hexagonal paving stones.
She seeks sensibility.
Removes her sunglasses
so the light may
violate the air.

Knobbed elms orbit
through her heart.
After winter skids
across the ice floes
she asks herself
where the days go.

These are the layers that make
the cake—the bright, red letters
of Nobody Beats the Wiz,
oxidized copper of distant statues,
the blue rattle that hushes her thoughts
and stokes the marrow.

The Dispossessed

Foundations riddle the pastoral.
Predictable geometry
tames the paisley
of wild fields—
the expansive horizon
breached by joist and lintel.
Desperate for a place to forage,
deer appear everywhere this summer—
a trio camps beneath
the moon's cold light,
scavenging from potato plot
what has eluded
the combine's efficiency.
Across Scuttlehole Road, house
frames rise like gallows.

Bracelet

Babies knock
just when the clock
of biology
has almost ceased its tautology.

An issue laid to rest
better not test
the roll of the dice
that wasn't so nice.

Take their advice
swallow the white pill.
Beware of sperm
that wiggle and squirm
and tear your house down.

Watch out for the maternity and hospital gown,
little children that make you frown.
No offspring either for sister Jill
(sexual preference rendered that possibility nil).

We're out here alone,
her with her lover, me with my man,
the past having died on its own—
no one left from that era to phone.
The future's an empty plate
hurled against the sky's pale slate.

Eggs come and go
murmuring of snow
each fleeting flake

separate, beautiful, aglow,
but Captain Bar Mitzvah and consort
reggaed on—the report
just beginning to filter in
on their comrades and kin.

You don't have to be a mother
to love another.
These babes inhabit this universe.
Better to loosen up than curse
my starkness,
be grateful for the chance
to be an honorary aunt,
let tenderness advance,
sadness no longer the final haunt.

Furious Abandon

A day wrapped in rain;
a fire that refuses
to ignite—all trails
lead to and from the storm.
The cat bites a sea shell.

Natural disaster blows
the roof right off.
The trees are topsy-turvy
on stately Ocean Road—
plucked like weeds
by God's hand.

Orange marigolds flame
in the returning sun.
Sing to us,
oh, Heavenly Father.
Paradise is even here and now.

The yard is plastered
with an oriental carpet
of brown and rust leaves.
Tell me, where do birds
go in a hurricane?

III

Death Takes A Holiday

I. *Featured Presentation: The Human Skeleton in*
Forensic Science

The unrecognized
necessitate
"before death" records
for positive identification.
Find a body in Tennessee,
call Dr. Bass.
The skull, a three-layered
sandwich: the spongy diploe
snug between hard inner
and outer bones of the cranium.
Sinuses as singular as fingerprints.

A burning body's extremities
are consumed first.
The head explodes
as gases build up.
A previous trauma
may cancel these
final pyrotechnics
by providing a portal
of release—a fracture,
small bullet hole,
will serve.

In the Washington/Adams Ballroom
slides flash black images—
torched vehicles,
abandoned souls,

a twelve-foot wall,
body at its base.
A capless bottle of hooch
tells Owen Rutherford's
tale: the Humpty Dumpty,
a tower of pallets
stacked as a stairway,
the second, fatal fall.

Two sisters remember being
forced to help their father
dig graves in the woods.
Call Dr. Bass to a particular
grove, study the soil.
It can never be replaced
as carefully as nature
first arranged it, small
disturbances in the pattern
of organic matter, rocks,
etc., cannot be avoided.
No apparent luxations—
the site blurred by time's
smudge, or false memory.

The volatile leach
of fatty acids can be used
to determine the time
of death, the dark stains test.
Nashville sods sets the hour
the deed was done.
Victim last seen leaving
downtown tavern at closing.

II. *Opryland Hotel Convention Center*

Fresh air dare not infiltrate
the maze of the Grand Ole
and brand new—an octopus
of rooms, corridors, levels
and forced nature.
Cascade Gardens, Delta Island
complete with flatboat ride,
four dollars American.
Magnolia Lobby, Verandah
Reflecting Pool, International
Airport 7 miles/11.26 kilometers
via Briley Parkway.

Real trees and hallelujah plants
inside a sealed compartment
in the Christmas countryside.
Lights strung in July
in hopes that bon vivants
"soon would be there."
Night shrouds the sky dome,
provisional bearings slip,
the garish turns spooky.

III. *The Nashville Committee has worked diligently to provide*
the ultimate professional experience . . .

THE BIOLOGICAL BASIS OF THINKING AND
LEARNING

Make two fists, place
knuckle against knuckle,
two hemispheres,
the thumbs as stem,

a perfect model.
Touch, sight, hearing
enter through the back.
On scans, we see neurons
explode like fireworks.
It takes motion for the gateway
to admit input from the eyes.

All images are broken
down and stored in separate
receptors. The yellow disc
becomes color, size,
shape, texture.

Photographic memory
does not exist.
Components reassemble
at the time of need.
Dendrite spines come and go
whispering "of Michelangelo."

Critical competitors
give us concepts.
Curiosity generates
new connectors.
Adrenaline produces stress
chemicals that prohibit
the formation of new links.

In the moment
of fear, of death,
we learn nothing.
Call Dr. Bass.

IV. *The Care and Feeding of Moon Rocks*

BECOME CERTIFIED TO RECEIVE *NASA* LUNAR
ROCKS AND REGOLITH SAMPLES

Mir astronauts can't see
an entire continent,
their range of vision limited
by lack of distance from Terra Firma.
They hover nine millimeters above
a standard twelve-inch globe.

The National Aeronautics
and Space Administration in order
to instruct America's children
will make available
samples of its beloved
lunar rocks to certain
certified, bona fide educators
provided the following
conditions are met:

> 1. Storage in a safe,
>   without any other high
>   theft valuables. Record
>   cards, clerical items
>   may share the sanctuary,
>   but not milk money, candy
>   sale proceeds, audio/video
>   equipment, etc.
> 2. Key locks may not be used.
> 3. Public display of lunar rocks
>   only in noncommercial areas.

4. Cannot be used to publicize
   the opening of a shoe
   store as one Florida teacher
   did in an effort to boost
   her husband's business.
   De-certification is deeply regretted
   but inevitable in such cases.

Notifying the local media
of the impeding
arrival of the samples
is strongly suggested.
Score one for our space program
and for all the little Neil Armstrongs
hankering to go aloft, their
appetite whetted by the fanfare
and moon pebbles (whoops, that is important,
unique specimens embedded—let
there be no flimflam—in a CD-
sized plastic disc).

There will never
be a full moon again.
In the event of the unthinkable
(theft or loss)—
call Mr. George Newby,
Marshall Flight Center, pronto.
Cool your heels, anticipate the F. B. I.

V. *Tennessee is a state rich in heritage and tradition. I hope you
will have the opportunity to take advantage of the many
attractions our state has to offer . . .*

Don Sundquist
Governor

The New York Delegation's
"on the road again . . ."
in white van courtesy
of Alamo Car Rental.
Music City's hometown
station announces Johnny
Cash has been admitted
to Nashville General
with advanced Parkinson's.
His voice resonates
from the deepest recesses
of Country's direct deposit system—
"Ring of Fire," "Folsom Prison Blues,"
        "Sea of Heartbreak."

The announcer's twang
further informs listeners
that the Reverend Billy Graham
has suffered a stroke
in the Sunshine State:
the Man in Black
and the man of God
in the same day.
Surfing channels one
October night,
we saw Johnny receive
his Presidential Gold Medal
at the Kennedy Center—
along with Bob Dylan,
Judith Jameison,
and others.
Cash was twitching
and jumping right out of his skin,
too much publicly acknowledged
substance abuse.

Stop to fuel vehicle—
Howard clambers out
to handle transaction.
Piercing screech emanates
from dashboard vicinity.
Neural transmitters in
full battle alert.
Vainly turn switches,
jiggle keys—must be
"Jew out of car alarm,
mandatory accessory
in Tennessee"—
just the eternal
conflict between low
beams and open doors.

Starbucks and the Gap
strut hand in hand—Nashville,
Pasadena, Soho, Boca.
We are everywhere and
nowhere. Big commerce
has designs on us.

Turn off US 231—
soft hills fold
around back roads; white cows
mimic sheep; solitary
low-slung wooden houses
look as though
the very air is too
much for them to support.
Climbing higher—
trees like frightened hairs
standing on end jut
from bare ridges; startling

cold and country light; sequins
of snow in the sun.
Vegetation, dun and reticent;
hills full of secrets.

VI. *Jack Daniel's Old Time Distillery*
   If you like eclectic science field trips, this is one you
   shouldn't miss!

Descend into Lynchburg
(Population 361), citizens with
tin pails stop traffic, solicit
donations for volunteer fire
department, provide clarification
of final directions to America's
oldest registered distillery,
founded 1866, in the bustle
of post-Civil-War reconstruction,
the perfect enterprise for
a wounded nation.

Evacuate van, cold squeezes
like a too tight glove.
Skip introductory film.
Benches like pews
set the proper, worshipful tone.
We've just made the next
tour, pile like circus clowns
into official minibus—
fellow pranksters include
two Texan couples, six
adolescents one step away
from lockup, and their counselor.
"Not that many places
around to take them on outings,"

he sheepishly acknowledges.
Which lesson—the joys
or the hazards of alcohol
consumption will be
assimilated in their
neural pathways?

First stop—warehouse
full of barrels for aging.
No smoking allowed,
the local brigade could never
be prepared for this
potential Armageddon.
Each cask is used
just once, then sold
to California vintners,
gives wine country
that Smoky Mountain undertone.
Move on to the blackened, massive
chimney where raw oak
becomes the briquettes
that will filter the final product—
only Jack and George Dickle
take this extra step.

Copper boilers, brass
pipes gleam—moonshine
as sanitized science;
golden seas of fermenting
grains—corn, wheat, barley;
industrial vats of percolation
and transmutation.
The longer it's left, the greater
the action—"bubble, bubble, toil and trouble . . ."
The new guided inquiry

kit, *Fermentation and Brewing*,
available for use in America's Constructivist
classrooms as we face the millennium.
Spumes erupt like Old Faithful.
"There's life in them thar hills."

Follow the red brick
road to a full-scale replica of the wizard
himself—standing, thanks to a solid marble
base, head and shoulders above
the common man—serene
as a saint while the underground
springs from which success emanated
emerge with a holy
babble of watery syllables.
Worldwide pilgrims
pay homage with a debonair
or desperate tilt of the bottle.
Brown crepe leaves pave Tennessee sod.

Next up, the cabin
where Jack had his office—
original desk and shelves littered
with wayward piles
of yellowed papers, formulations
and calculations fading.
(No such thing as photographic memory.)
Here sits the squat,
square safe whose failure
to cooperate so aggrieved
our hero that it elicited
the kick that resulted in the once,
by all accounts, healthy tissue
of his big toe, left foot
falling victim to trauma-

induced obstruction of circulation,
the creeping gangrene
that went unnoticed
(dare we suggest,
as the result of too much
quality control sampling
of the aforementioned
brown gold?) till death snuck
in, and he was as cold
as his marble likeness.
Call Dr. Bass's predecessor, pronto.

The tour agenda quickly moves
from the macabre (we want the
day trippers titillated but not given
to second thoughts about
the wisdom of consumption)
to the barrels where those earlier
highlighted briquettes are put
to use. "We can't offer you
any samples, Moore being a dry county,
but allow me to crack the lid
a bit. Open your lips. Let
the fumes hit the roof
of your mouth and just swallow."
Sensations—liquid, strong,
sweet, all explode as condensation
defeats local edict.

Then it's off to the White Rabbit
Saloon for ambiance, if not imbibing.
Enticingly packed decanters
of Gentleman Jack,
seventy-five dollars a pop,
available in the anteroom

for enjoyment elsewhere.
The matter of lunch
remains to be dealt with—our
guide recommends a spot
back in Lynchburg.
The town square rings
with the sound of caroling.
Souvenir shops line the perimeter.
They contain every possible variation
of beverage container—mug, shot
glass, decanter, clear, smoked,
black, etc.—and an equally impressive
assortment of vestments—T-shirts, ties,
sweatshirts, all emblazoned
with the holy insignia, not
to mention the toothpick
holders, dish towels and napkin
rings that have made Jack
the Martha Stewart of Tennessee.

Seated in the back room, menus
passed around, when who should
appear but the very Texas couples
we've so recently separated from.
What symbiosis exists between
the White Rabbit Saloon
and the Grand Garden Cafe?
In the dead space where desires
are expressed and hungers
are not yet satisfied they engage
us in idle chitchat. Howard,
ever the gentleman, explains
the rationale for our presence—
the educational vanguard we
represent, National Science Foundation

funding, team building and so on.

We have been disarmed
by the woman's drawl,
so that her derringer fires
with the intended
surprise: "What is your
ethnic background?
Are you all Germans?"
She trains her imperious gaze
on each of us, demanding
a confirmation of her suspicions
that she has been seated
in a nest of New York Jews,
or a pedigree proving otherwise.
The spotlight works
its way around
the table. I hear the inane,
shocked, even polite
recitations of my fellow facilitators.

Will I answer or refuse?
Go for the equally offensive
paternal Polish Catholic
family tree, or trot out my mother's
Daughters of the American Revolution
forebears—the Sands
family, lineage traced
back to 1410 England—
proud poets and scholars
(mess with us not, ask
Mary Queen of Scots)?
They were present at
beheadings, the founding
of colonies—Block

Island, Virginia, Sands Point—
patriots of the Revolutionary War—
gave America its first
poet, George Sandys.

All this time Howard
is enmeshed in an effort
of civility with our friends
from the Longhorn State,
his head and body
turned away from our table.
The waitress approaches
with our tray of vittles—chili,
stuffed baked potatoes, hamburgers and beverages.

Bite your tongue,
bite your burger.
All the mad cows
have sponges for brains.

VII. *Stones River*

> *Take your gun and go, John,*
> *Take your gun and go.*
> *For Ruth can drive the oxen,*
> *And I can use the hoe.*
>
> **Civil War song**

Off again, our escape
a success, even if we
almost collide with a red pickup
as Howard exits the town square
in a trajectory
directly contradictory
to the "One-Way" arrows.

The road back is
long and filled with choices.
Guidebooks consulted—
we head for the Stones River
Civil War Battlefield and Union Cemetery,
but first set our sights
on the Web School,
a preparatory academy
whose brochure brags
that it has " produced ten
Rhodes Scholars and the governors
of three states" and recommends to
"Leave at least an hour for your visit."

Relieved to have
a destination, to be able
to put the recent past behind,
we circumnavigate back roads,
cross railroad tracks,
pass through towns
in the blink of an eye.
Finally, Bell Buckle—
the symbols found carved
on a beech tree by the creek
to mark grazing lands—
site of the Web School.
One room full of memorabilia,
glass cases filled with photos,
medals and athletic trophies.
We complete our tour
well within the recommended hour.
Heading back to Nashville, the bucolic
yielding to the ever more populous.
Functional buildings bespeak
the common culture's assertive hand.

West on US 41, then the Old
Nashville Highway in Mufreesboro
to Stones River National Park.
Ignorant of particular events,
but not of the Civil War itself
with all its implications.
> *In Flanders fields the poppies blow*
> *Between the crosses, row on row . . .*

Tommy Barry blown to bits
dismantling a land mine, Vietnam.

Where have all the flowers gone?
Gone to soldiers everyone.

Iraq—SCUD missiles as pac-man
on twilight TV.

I ain't gonna practice war no more.

Driving into the historic site, past
regimented white tombstones,
abandoned battlefields,
on to the visitors' center—slick, modern
technology contrasting with original relics.
Push a button, hear a treatise
on cannon loading—then the awful,
reproduced roar.

83,000 fought
23,000 died here—
four hundred acres,
one tenth the actual battlefield
preserved in their memory.

December 4, 1997—
the sun low on the meadow
painting everything crimson as it decamps.

The Union debacle at Fredricksburg
in mid-December. The rebel
army dancing on the American
flag at holiday balls.
Great Britain's threatened intervention.
Lincoln's growing anger; depression.
The necessity to halt
Bragg's Confederate forces.

Christmas Eve 1862
Rosecrans issues orders
to advance—"Press them hard,
Drive them from their nests!
Make them fight or run!
Fight them. Fight them I say!"

Drenching rains, roads
turned to swamps, campfires
prohibited, can't even get
a hot cup of coffee.

Burned homes,
chimneys like grave markers,
rickety wagons, fleeing refugees
driving livestock before them.

December 30th—the two sides
so close they hear
the jingling of each
others' canteens, the metallic
clash of rifles.

Challenging each other
with patriotic songs—
    "Dixie," "The Bonnie Blue Flag" versus "Yankee
        Doodle," "Hail Columbia."
"Home Sweet Home" picked up by both sides.
In the misty half light
10,000 Confederates attack
while the Union troops
are eating breakfast.
    " . . . swooped down on those Yankees
    like a whirl-a-gust of woodpeckers
    in a hail storm."
Frying pans sizzling
with eggs no one would eat.
The "sip-sip" of bullets
clipping mangled cedar trees.

9 A.M.—under devastating fire
for three hours, Rosecrans
on his gray charger, shouting: "This
battle must be won!"
The Union lines bend
into a V, 50 cannons
turn on the Rebels.

5 P.M.— attacks cease,
night falls—
7,000 Federals
and an equal number
of Confederates
dead or wounded.
That night proved
so cold that many
were frozen to the ground
by their own blood.

The next day, one
last attempt by Bragg.
The deafening roar
of well-placed artillery.
In one hour 1,700 Rebels die.

The Union claims victory
by virtue of holding the ground.
The Emancipation Proclamation
passed into law January 1
while the armies were still
bleeding and dying.

Lincoln writes to Rosecrans:
"I can never forget, whilst
I remember anything . . . you
gave us a hard-earned victory,
which, had there been a
defeat instead, the nation
could scarcely have lived over."

We exit the visitors center,
confront the sweep of quiet
fields, mowed grass, clumps
of cedars, solitary cannons—
sculptural and innocent.
It is December, the sun falling
just as it did one hundred
and thirty-five years ago.
The screams of the dead
and wounded dissolve in thin air.
Withered leaves sprinkle the ground
where the soldiers surrendered their lives.
We tramp across the field,
stand behind a single cannon

and try to imagine what it was like.
The Civil War is still a reality
down here in a way
it has ceased to be
back North.

The sky-banded stratus
clouds—blue, gray, white,
tinged with the palest pink
as though all that
old blood had soaked
into the sky. The light
begins to fail, but we are still
compelled to patrol
the rows of tombstones,
their white faces glowing
in the near dark,
as though by facing each one
we could comprehend, pay
homage to the boys
whispering from the ground.
Saddened here in the raw cold
of another year's end
there are no jokes, no tears, no prejudices.

Dr. Bass has dogged our steps
from the lecture
in the Grand Ole Opry Ballroom
to the major's skull
that splattered
blood and brains across
General Rosecrans's tunic.

Look for evidence
among the synapses,
the bent hairs and lunar
memories embedded
in plastic discs for safekeeping.
The eye that doesn't move
acknowledges no input—denies
access to both past and future—
data entry possible
only if there is motion.

We look skyward—each of us
with silent thoughts—
a final benediction before
piling back into the van.

VIII. *Epilogue*

Thursday, April 16, 1998
TWISTER TERROR SWEEPS NASHVILLE

It looked just like the Wizard of Oz.
My feet felt like they were floating off the floor.
Margret Mahler
Department of Transportation worker

That sky blanches gray,
then lavender.
All goes still.
3 P.M., lights out.

Two-thirds of the city without power.
Estimated damage: 100 million dollars.

Continuous network coverage.
Along the Cumberland River
in downtown Nashville,
a building we'd strolled past
on the way to our final
Central Time Zone dinner
totally demolished.
A pickup truck
blown upside down
in front of Music City Lounge.

"It's really unsafe . . . there are a lot
of things hanging from buildings."
Phil Bredesen, Mayor

> Tornadoes are rated by the single
> most intense example of damage.

The Fujiti Scale: A human risk
analysis tool, named for Professor
Ted Fujiti. (He was part of the team
that investigated Hiroshima and
Nagasaki—the shadows burned in
by an atomic fireball can be used
to determine the exact blast-height
and position of the bomb.)

> F 0 - tree branches snap
> F 1 - damages mobile home siding
> F 2 - well-built barn destroyed
> F 3 - throws vehicles
> F 4 - walls and roofs demolished
> F 5 - well-constructed home completely swept
> away, only the foundation remains

Winds can range from 72 mph to 318 mph.
Nashville tornado is given an F 5 rating.

The false lights of the Grand
Ole Opry Hotel beckon
down corridors where
ordinary folks dream.
Science, education,
medicine, faith
(old-fashioned and New Age):
all part of the struggle
not to perish.

The arrogance of geography—
New York buildings
molt their skins
like snakes.
One University Place—
a pediment falls,
crashes through a windshield.
Now scaffolding
surrounds the building.

This week, new eruptions
in the war against cancer.
Frogs vanishing
at alarming rate.
Scientific summit called.
CAUTION: animal model
not always applicable to human.
Gone "postal" becomes
gone "school"—
white boys with guns.

A crucial bolt
fails in Yankee Stadium,
concrete crushes empty seats.
Mayor says he can raise
one billion dollars
for new sports palace,
congratulates Governor
for vetoing the money
for school repairs.
"It was the fiscally
responsible thing to do."
Walls tumble—
Yan Zhan Zhao killed
going to pick up her
siblings at P. S. 131, Brooklyn.

The failure
of the cranium
to protect.
Ask General Bragg.
Ask Rosecrans.
Call Dr. Bass.

IV

Cloud Town

Our case is not
   the worst case.
        There are obscure paths
           in
           clear
              matters.

                Shrouds of clouds.
                Haloes of clouds.

   Clouds recall the parapets
before geometry,

          deserve neither pleasure nor censure.

              Iron clouds meditate
              on the scarlet cardinal.

Zeus formed Nephele
from clouds as a counterfeit Hera.

           Each cloud requires
           its own analogy.

           The theater of the
             w i n d
           complicates migration.

   Dogs run up the hayfield road,
inhaling and exhaling cloud,
vanish into even grayness.

Cloudiness is measured
in tenths—a sky three-tenths,
or less, clouded is considered clear.

Clouds like repeating memories.

The average U. S. rate
of cloudiness is fifty percent,
or we receive fifty percent of the
possible sunlight.

That first flight through
the belly of a cloud, the surprising solidity.

Who will save us from ourselves?

In aviation, the base
of the layer is the ceiling.

The three anatomical shapes—
                    Cumulus
                              Stratus
                                   Cirrus.

The diversity within each—
  Orographic clouds shaped
by the mountains;
Mammatus smoothly pebbled
  as a low-water beach;
Pileus, the skullcap.

Clouds, the great
impostors.

Other shifts defy appraisal.
Altitude, direction, velocity
are not fiction.

Particles smaller than 0.5 microns
zigzag continuously
in random directions . . .

Cloud droplets serve as gathering spots
for these wayward specks. On contact
they adhere
or sink in and dissolve.

Clouds kiss
the prairie.

In the clouds
On a cloud
Under a cloud
Beclouded

The ephemeral onslaught.

In the cloud chamber
all is revealed.

Impossible not to know.

The Burgeoning Buds

The famous tree
traces a doily of shade.
A tiny bird taps
gray and fractured bark
while the white-ringed
pheasant patrols the border.
Daffodils and violets
compete for first-color-
of-the-season honors.

The pond awaits the offspring
of the mallard whose trust
has been carefully cultivated.
Patient labor has coaxed
hills and hidden paths
from formerly flat fields.
Freshly painted porch columns
shimmer in the sun,
illustrate the difference
between white and light.

I cannot help but fear
the approaching summer
without the pacifier of nature,
the rhythm of the countryside.
I tremble a year
after the initial event—
like a Vietnam vet suffering
delayed stress reaction.
The underbrush ricochets
with unidentified vibrations.

I want to lose myself in the soft
belly of the atmosphere.
In the herb garden
a miniature saint
beseeches all passersby.
A snapping turtle surfaces
in the pond, ready
like disaster to bite
without provocation.

In summer the maze of plants
bends the arrow of vision,
making the property
appear smaller than it is.
Only in a more barren season
are the actual dimensions revealed—
when full of green distractions,
we remain unaware of the real
magnitude of its proportions.

Explornography

There is no denouncement,
only the tease of a glimmer,
the hope of letting go
when all else fails.
Grief's vertigo skulks,

like the jut of the moraine's
hammered spine along
the plains of the South Fork,
unacknowledged, but inevitable—
given the glacial pull
of our collective geology.

The Photographer

All summer he watches deer
emerge just as the sun begins
its descent behind silver birches.
Each night he inches closer—
he wants them accustomed to his presence.
One rash step will send them
bounding back into the woods,
destroying the picture
slowly developing in his mind.
He observes the strong curve
of the stag's head
silhouetted in falling light;
how antlers repeat the angles
of branches overhead;
how each living thing molds
the space that surrounds it.

Gravity

for William Fener

Billy's dead.
All birds have the same form
but differ much
in size and shape of parts.

Billy's dead.
His '69 Pontiac motored through Canada, Tennessee,
    the Skyline Drive.
Migrating flocks follow river valleys,
coastlines, mountain chains.

Billy's dead.
Impossible to overfeed
fledglings—their throats
refuse to work when sated.

Billy's dead.
Birds' hearts beat twice
as fast as humans'.
They can be near or farsighted at will.

Billy's dead.
"Cheerily, cheerily, cheer up,"
calls the robin. Lighthouses lure
unlucky flocks to their deaths.

Billy's dead.
The hollow bones of birds
support great weight.
Fate waits to bake sparrows in a pie.

Billy's dead.
Pure white eggs laid
in dark places. Judge
the blue jay by deeds alone.

Billy's dead.
Its tail is a rudder
to guide flight and landings.
He plunged ahead without instrumentation.

Billy's dead.
I can't get it into my head.
Birds' bills may be trowels, chisels, augers.
Billy's dead.

Breviary

Unrecalled yellows,
forsythia and daffodils
like humble flashes
against thunderstruck fields.
In the side woods, cream
petals notched
with a bruise of pink.

Not a leaf is still,
but all are secure
on their branches.
The sky, mauve blotting paper
with fountain-pen-ink clouds.
Write yourself a letter, seal it
with a smudge of morning glory.

The Roman Pool

Pleasure is worth what you can afford to pay for it.
William Randolph Hearst

It is cold and deeply blue
down here. Pumps bring water
and a salted chill from the ocean
miles away. The walls and floor
are set with squares of tile,
cobalt faced with gold; laid
in echoing complexities
by artisans imported to complete
this underground amusement.

There are statues white and Greek,
promises of gods and heroes
whose muscles seem to move
in this nocturnal precinct.
Boilers rage incessantly,
but still this pool provides
a bracing baptism too austere
for him. He never swims
inside this chamber.

Prefers the Neptune Pool,
twice enlarged, where the sun
heats mountain springs,
and bushes bloom in perfect life,
the dead ones clipped and gone
before he rises. He leaves
this pleasure to those that serve him.
What vexes him, delights those
accustomed to simpler expectations.

Dialogue on the Two Chief Systems

Galileo saw the blazing center,
the one body around which the earth
and her eight sisters spin.

> This is the first statement.
> How to do it is not clear.

It is the sun
to which the planets cling,
not reassuring theories.

> The policemen, like all the rest,
> are concerned about their families.

One man read another
and did not believe him

> We have come in numbers so large
> that the message must get through.

until distant light gathered
into one clear image,
a stationary star, a waltzing globe.

> The world, the end of the world,
> the fight against the end.

Exiled to Arcetri; ordered
not to write or teach,

> Watch what they do.

he rose from his knees
to whisper, "Eppur si muove,"
"Yet it moves."

Escape

Falling down the rabbit
hole and through
the looking glass—
Alice, Alice
the Queen is mad.
The hare holds
medical instruments.

Tweedle-dee and Tweedle-dum
sing heavenly hymns.
Off with their heads,
arms, legs
counsels the sage.
Doctor Death haunts
the Wisconsin woods.

Flee, flee reason screams.
This can't be happening.
It's my party and I'll cry
if I want to.
(Miss my mother, want
her sweet embrace
before the storm.)

Five minutes of breathtaking
snow outside
the thermopane window,
then sunlight like God's
golden paintbrush—
changes nothing,
changes everything.

Midterm in Harlem

A certain authority mixed
with innocence—too much
honesty can ruin you.
The Old Kingdom, the Middle Kingdom,

the New Kingdom—
the pharaohs wait
wrapped in linen, heart
and brain in separate jars,

while the ordinary lie sideways
in the sand. Aqua gum in one mouth;
violet, pink and jade in others.
One, two jaws snap with precision.

Whole sentences begin and end,
"late again?" The struggle is to convince
us to pound the reeds.
Abandon all gods save Aton

of the Sun. The geranium still blooms,
though there is a tendency
for the Nile to flood her banks.
Dark rivulets fertilize the windowsill.

What We Know

for Genevieve

Not the distant pediments of trees,
not the dangling oranges,
not the palm fronds.
No bird dares the sky.
Nothing is moving.

All is
dust beneath
the sienna mantle.
Clouds swell
then darken—
take on a gray shape
of their own.
The atmosphere chafes.

Still, as museum specimens,
we can only hope to move on.
Pressed like butterflies
between pages of a book,
we can only try to recall.

Whose Experiment

I.

The genesis of the roadblock
is perverse—old, reliable fence
proof of its existence.
Only the cat makes us
resolute as Bay of Fundy
riptides funnel
through the living room.
There are orchestrations afoot
we neither desire nor comprehend.

II.

After Oklahoma City
to walk past Federal Plaza
in Manhattan is an act
of contrived innocence.
Today they gave up the search—
safety of the surely living
weighed against twelve-day odds,
as chunks of concrete
quarrel in prairie winds.

III.

Washington Square Park asserts
itself beyond windows
restored by a professional.
Urban conversation ricochets
off the created pastoral.
Chores help avoid the inevitable.
The brain constructs
a thousand chambers, fully
booked for the duration.

IV.

Beneath the collapsed Sampoong
department store a young woman
waited nineteen days—leading
to new adjustments in how
long searchers must persist.
She knew she would live
because in a dream
a monk came to her
and gave her an apple.

V.

Across the divide
of Waverly Place,
rain-ignited winds tatter
the purple university banner.
Inside 3E, Richter's
once-heard/always-recognizable
notes whisk varnished air—
as his Schubert orders
our souls not to surrender.

Halation

JANUARY 6

Winter light cuts with the precision of an old-fashioned
tin cookie cutter. The sky above the park is a pale, brave
flicker of blue. Everyone walks with a mission, dedicated
dog owners the only strollers. The motors of cars, hushed
as if they too have no energy to spare in random racket.

JANUARY 7

A blizzard of ferocity unseen since 1888 muffles the coun-
try. Flakes fly with Jackson Pollock abandon. The black
iron railings of Washington Square Park are being sucked
into the white quicksand. Street lights, triggered by
storm-snuffed darkness, ignite their mandarin globes. A
brave or foolish car digs out. Fifteen minutes later, what
had been bare asphalt beneath its belly is one with the
surrounding couture. Solitary pedestrians stumble like
drunks.

JANUARY 8

States of emergency flesh out the Northeast map. Cobalt
slap of lightening against room-darkening window
shades. 3 A. M. buses cease running after six fall victim to
impossible drifts. Cabin fever racks confined muscles. A
short walk procures one ice scraper and Amoson. Happy
to see Posman's Books open, someone will feed the two
resident cats. Ours glories in the extra attention.

JANUARY 9

The exhilaration of purity. Pigeon colony at the Arch,
gray against George Washington's bleached and crum-
bling facade. Governor Whitman recounts how state

troopers had to bring people to dialysis. Cold shiver of past, machine-dependent existence. Glorious, gold sun before the gathering dark. 7:30 P. M. fragile fall of additional flakes.

January 10 and 11

20.2 inches of snow reduces to 1.3 of plain rain. Apartment, Siberia, no fuel delivery possible. Worry about cold cat. Reality check, street cats survive much worse. Still, she does not like the chilled Bridgehampton fall and spring, slinks around low to the ground like a heat-seeking missile. The urban, particulate air reveals its content on unscrolled parchment.

January 13

35 degrees feels like a heat wave. Curbs disappear under a flood of melting snow. City garbage pickup resumes tomorrow. Black plastic bags are stacked like logs outside service entrances.

January 15

Beneath the window, giant snow-loading machinery roars like a day-glow orange dragon. White dump trucks line up to receive winter's communion. The furrowed street pleats like a farmer's field.

January 19

Night descends at 2:45 P. M. while trees of lightning snake down obscured skies. Barbara Jordan of Texas dies. She always carried a copy of the Constitution in her handbag. A good soaking by a powerful thunderstorm was all that was needed to flush away the remaining embankments. Ellen Adler trots by with her tiny dog stuffed in its red knit coat.

Microscopic flakes that have no staying power. They dust, then disappear like dream thoughts that seem lucid till we wake.

Photo by Iannis Delatolas

About the Author

SUSAN BARAN was born and raised in New York City. She is the author of *Harmonious Whole* (Groundwater Press, 1989). She was the founder and director of the Intuflo Reading Series. She teaches science and literature at the Emily Dickinson School, and lives in Manhattan and Sag Harbor.